TOP 200 Smoothie Recipes C

Written by: Jamie Stewart

Copyright © 2015

All Rights Reserved

Warning-Disclaimer

***

Download a FREE PDF file with photos of all the recipes. Link located at the end of the book

***

Table of Contents

Introduction

Do you make your healthy smoothies on a daily basis from habit? Do you even have a blender in your kitchen? If you are looking for a new way to eat healthier and better, this cookbook can be your great inspiration and a useful guide to the world of blending and juicing.

Making a juicy and delicious smoothie is a great way to provide your family with some nutrient-rich foods such as vegetables, fruits, nuts, etc. If you do not already have this healthy habit, after reading this book, you will include the smoothies in your daily meal plan, perhaps. See for yourself, "200 Smoothie Recipes" will make your blending a breeze!

Just three magic words –Unprocessed, Unsweetened, Natural

Smoothie is just as good as whole ingredients such as a whole apple, whole carrot or a glass of milk. Meal replacement smoothie is an important source of plant fiber, antioxidants and the other very useful nutrition. If you are in a hurry, you can drink your smoothie whenever you want, at any time of the day, in any occasion. You do not have to sit at the table, chewing your fruit or vegetables. You can simply take your meal with you. You can find simply recipes for a fruity start to the day in "200 Smoothie Recipes" cookbook. Then, you will find vegetable smoothies, which are the perfect snack between main meals, or simply and healthy dinner. When should you usually drink your favorite smoothie? Actually, there is no rule.

Breakfast in the glass.

It sounds great for all the busy people who do not have time to have a breakfast.

I feel like having a snack. Healthy and refreshing brunch.

No problem! Simply put some fruit or vegetables in your blender and just in a few minutes you will get a complete vitamin meal.

Meal-replacement smoothie for dinner.

Yummy! It sounds so delicious, so good. Many of us do not like big, "heavy" dinner. Smoothie is a perfect dinner because it contains a lot of water that hydrates our body during the night. Then, it contains vitamins, minerals, and omega-3 fatty acids that nourish our body.

Post-Exercise Smoothies.

Well-balanced, right smoothie can help in energy supply and recovery after your workout, by providing essential electrolytes, carbs, protein, fatty acids and so on. Regardless of whether you make your post-workout smoothie or your meal-replacement smoothie, make sure that you're using a high-quality ingredients. You should use high-quality protein food such as yogurt, almond milk, Whey Protein, Soy Protein and so on. Add some fruits and vegetables and you will be full of energy. Smoothie is one of the best food to eat (drink) before and after a workout.

If you deplete your body with intense training almost every day, make sure that you fuel your body with the highest quality foods. The consistent juicing regimen provides you with many benefits for overall health.

Try to use the fresh ingredients in order to get the nutrient from the whole foods as well as the fiber from the fruit and vegetable skin. Organic food is even better, but local and chemical-free is the best for you.

Eight Top Reasons to Consume Smoothies Every Day

I'm not sure that I take enough vitamins and minerals. What am I supposed to do?

You no longer have to worry about your daily needs for nutrients. Fortunately, making your own homemade smoothie gives you the ability to control your nutrition. You can calculate the amount of calories and the amount of UH, proteins, vitamins, minerals as well as the other nutritional facts. For example, Strawberry Banana Smoothie per one serving size contains 121 calories. Then, it contains UH 10% (28.8g), Vitamin A 10%, Vitamin C 45%, Dietary Fiber 5% (1.3g), Protein 5% (1.3g) and so on. There are a huge number of Nutrition Facts Tables (NFT) on the Internet and all the information are readily available to you.

As a matter of fact, simply follow easy and quick recipes from this cookbook. These recipes contain the best combination of various ingredients that can provide you with essential nutrients.

"200 Smoothie Recipes" can teach you good eating habits.

People who have a healthy habit of drinking of smoothies, they pay attention to what they usually eat. When you begin to practice this healthy habit, your entire psycho-physical condition will change for the better. Better digestion, faster metabolism, more balanced blood sugar levels, reduction of the risk of cancer…Your hair and nails will be beautiful, strong and healthy. Your skin will become healthier, rejuvenated and refreshed. And you suddenly realize that healthy habits make sense! Now, your cup is half full and your life is amazing!

How can I get my child to eat more vegetables and fruits?

This is the common question. A lot of parents are concerned that their children don't get enough vitamins and minerals from vegetables and fruits. There is one more common problem that can be summarized in one sentence: "Help! My child doesn't want to drink a milk!"

Smoothie is a perfect way to end their picky eating. Simply mix up a meal or snack in less than 5 minutes and your child will have a glass of delicious healthy drink. Please read "200 Smoothie Recipes" and give it a try.

You are able to supply your body and mind with more energy.

There are many reasons that lead to the weakening of our health. Stressful lifestyle, unhealthy habits such as smoking, overweight, getting older, etc. Poor memory, anxiety, brain fog and depression are the signs that your brain isn't getting the right nutrients. For example, the apples contain "quercetin" that protects your brain from diseases such as Alzheimer's. Of course, you will find a lot of inspiring and creative smoothie recipes that contain the apples in "200 Smoothie Recipes".

Fortunately, there are the super foods that can help you maintain the health of your body and mind such as smoothies!

You need simple kitchen equipment and minimalist kitchen.

Everything you need to create the perfect smoothies does not take up a lot of space in the kitchen. What do you need?

A great cookbook with a huge collection of smoothie recipes.

A blender or some smoothie maker to suit your budget.

Cutting boards for chopping your fresh ingredients.

Solid chef's knife.

Sharp paring knife (for opening fruits with hard rinds)

Wooden or plastic spatula.

Glass or plastic jars for storing.

Simply combine a variety of fruits, add your favorite vegetables and a little milk. Done! The smoothies could seriously save you time in the kitchen. Actually, making healthy smoothie on a daily basis is easier than you think.

If you need to lose weight, you have the solution at your fingertips!

You can lose weight easier than ever before with "200 Smoothie Recipes". Here you will find a huge number of smoothies that are low in calories. At the same time, these smoothies are so delicious and they give you a feeling of fullness, so you will lose weight easily. Forget starvation diets, enjoy the healthy smoothies, relax, and drop your pounds. Just follow a few simple rules and you will improve.

When choosing the smoothies from this cookbook, avoid recipes that contain sugar, ice cream, whipped cream, chocolate and similar ingredients. Choose rather vegetables than fruits, water than milk, and low fat dairy products instead of plain milk, whole yogurt or full-fat cheese. When choosing your ingredients for a smoothie, try to eat a variety of colors. Shoot especially for greens, because they're the richest in free radical-fighting antioxidants.

This is a great low-cost way to eat healthy.

You can make the smoothies directly from the comfort of your kitchen. You can use almost any fruits and vegetables you have in the kitchen. The possibilities are limitless. Choose local and seasonal fruits and vegetables and you will stay on budget.

Easy, quick and fun!

You do not need any special culinary skills to prepare a great smoothie! Even the children can make the smoothies. You can make amazing smoothie with only 2 to 3 ingredients. In this cookbook, you will find easy recipes with ingredients that everyone can afford. Anyway, feel free to substitute any of your favorite ingredients. Experiment and let your imagination fly! Have a fun! Think about some spices that can add a nice touch to your smoothies. You can throw a great party with alcoholic smoothies, too. Brighten up your party with creamy and refreshing alcoholic and non-alcoholic smoothies.

Everyone has own reasons, but all of the reasons can be summarized in the same thing – the smoothies are just too yummy!

Try this, join millions of people around the world who enjoy smoothies every day.

Apple Orange Smoothie

(Ready in about 5 minutes | Servings 2)

Ingredients

2 cups apple sauce

1 cup apple cider

1 cup orange juice

2 tablespoon maple syrup

1/4 teaspoon ground nutmeg

1/2 teaspoon ground cinnamon

Directions

Combine all ingredients in a blender. Pulse until the mixture is smooth.

Pour into 2 glasses and serve immediately.

Apple Banana Smoothie

(Ready in about 10 minutes | Servings 2)

Ingredients

2 ripe bananas, peeled and quartered

2 apples, peeled, cored and quartered

10 fluid ounces nonfat yogurt

2 tablespoons honey

15 fluid ounces soy milk

Directions

Put all of the ingredients in an electric blender or a food processor.

Purée for 1 minute. Transfer to the glasses and serve over ice cubes.

Super Energy Apple Smoothie

(Ready in about 10 minutes | Servings 2)

Ingredients

3/4 cup apple sugar-free syrup

1/4 cup cinnamon sugar-free syrup

2 scoops Vege Fuel

1 1/2 cups crushed ice

1/4 cup heavy cream

Ground cinnamon for garnish

Directions

Place all ingredients in your blender.

Purée until well blended and smooth.

Transfer the smoothie to the glasses. Sprinkle cinnamon over the top and serve immediately.

Banana Peach Smoothie

(Ready in about 10 minutes | Servings 2)

Ingredients

2 frozen ripe bananas

1 cup peach nectar

1/2 cup milk

1 tablespoon sunflower seeds

Directions

Place all ingredients in a blender. Cover and blend until smooth.

Serve with ice cubes.

Peanut Butter Banana Smoothie

(Ready in about 5 minutes | Servings 1)

Ingredients

1 cup skim milk

1/2 banana, peeled

1 tablespoon peanut butter

1 teaspoon high-fructose corn syrup

5 ice cubes

Directions

In a blender, mix milk, banana, peanut butter and corn syrup.

Add ice cubes and pulse until smooth. Serve immediately.

Banana Raspberry Smoothie

(Ready in about 5 minutes | Servings 1)

Ingredients

1 frozen banana, peeled

1/4 cup frozen raspberries

1 tablespoon peanut butter

1 cup orange juice

3 tablespoons vanilla yogurt

Directions

In a blender or a food processor, combine all ingredients.

Cover and mix until smooth. Serve cold.

Strawberry Banana Smoothie

(Ready in about 10 minutes | Servings 1)

Ingredients

1 frozen banana, peeled

1/4 cup fresh strawberries

1/2 cup orange juice

5 tablespoons strawberry yogurt

Directions

In a blender or a food processor, combine all ingredients.

Cover and pulse a few times until the mixture becomes smooth. Garnish with fresh strawberries and banana slices and serve.

Vegan Power Smoothie

(Ready in about 5 minutes | Servings 2)

Ingredients

1 cup nonfat soy milk

1/2 cup orange juice

1 banana

1/2 cup cantaloupe

1 teaspoon peanut butter

1/2 cup fresh or frozen strawberries

Frozen cantaloupe balls for garnish (optional)

Directions

Place all ingredients in a blender container. Put lid on tightly.

Pulse until smoothie consistency is reached. Garnish with frozen cantaloupe balls (optional) and serve.

Blueberry Vanilla Smoothie

(Ready in about 5 minutes | Servings 3)

Ingredients

2 cups vanilla yogurt

2 bananas, peeled

10 blueberries

1/2 teaspoon almond extract

1 tablespoon sugar or sugar substitute

Chopped almonds for garnish

Directions

In a blender, place all ingredients and pulse until the mixture gets smooth consistency.

Pour your smoothie in 4 glasses. Sprinkle the almonds over the top and serve immediately.

Chocolate Fruit Smoothie

(Ready in about 5 minutes | Servings 2)

Ingredients

2 bananas, frozen and chunked

1/2 cup frozen strawberries

2 tablespoons chocolate syrup

1 cup plain yogurt

1 tablespoon sunflower seeds

Directions

In a blender, place all ingredients.

Blend until smooth and serve immediately.

Apple Coconut Smoothie

(Ready in about 10 minutes | Servings 1)

Ingredients

1/4 cup apple juice

1/2 teaspoon coconut, grated

1/2 banana

1/4 teaspoon fresh ginger root, grated

2 small ice cubes

Directions

Put all ingredients into your blender.

Blend until smoothie consistency is reached. Pour into glass, top with shredded coconut (optional) and serve.

Fruit and Oatmeal Breakfast Smoothie

(Ready in about 5 minutes | Servings 2)

Ingredients

1 cup soy milk

1/2 cup rolled oats

1 banana, quartered

14 frozen strawberries

1 tablespoon sugar (optional)

Directions

Blend soy milk, oats, banana, and strawberries until smooth.

Add the sugar (optional) and lightly blend until incorporated. Serve.

Strawberry and Asian Pear Shake

(Ready in about 10 minutes | Servings 2)

Ingredients

1 Asian pear, cored and sliced

2 large strawberries

2/3 cup strawberry yogurt

1/4 cup fat-free milk

2 teaspoons white sugar

1 tablespoon sunflower seeds

4-5 ice cubes

Directions

Place all of the ingredients into a blender.

Process until thick and smooth.

Pour into chilled glasses and serve.

Apricot Mango Smoothie

(Ready in about 5 minutes | Servings 1)

Ingredients

6 ounces light Apricot-Mango yogurt

1 cup Crystal Light lemonade

1/2 banana

6 canned apricot halves

Directions

Puree all ingredients in a blender until smooth and thick, or 1 to 2 minutes.

Serve immediately.

Blueberry Kale Smoothie

(Ready in about 5 minutes | Servings 1)

Ingredients

1½ cups almond milk, unsweetened

1 small frozen banana

1 cup frozen blueberries

1 cup chopped kale

4-5 walnuts

2 teaspoons honey

Directions

Purée all ingredients in a blender until smooth, or 1 to 2 minutes.

Serve immediately. You can add a little water in order to bring your smoothie to a drinkable consistency.

Green Tea Fruit Smoothie

(Ready in about 15 minutes | Servings 2)

Ingredients

3 tablespoons water

1 green tea bag

2 teaspoon honey

1½ cups blueberries

1 small banana

3/4 cup light vanilla soy milk

Directions

To make the green tea: Microwave water until steaming hot. Add tea bag and allow to stand for 3 minutes. Remove tea bag.

Add honey to the prepared tea and stir to combine.

Blend tea, fruit and soy milk until the mixture is smooth. Serve chilled.

Almond Kale Smoothie

(Ready in about 5 minutes | Servings 1)

Ingredients

1 small frozen banana, diced

3/4 cup kale, stems removed

3/4 cup almond milk

1 teaspoon almond butter

1/8 teaspoon cinnamon

1/8 teaspoon ground ginger

Directions

Place ingredients into your blender.

Pulse until all ingredients are incorporated or for 2 minutes.

Pour in a tall glass and enjoy!

Nectarine Apricot Smoothie

(Ready in about 5 minutes | Servings 1)

Ingredients

1/2 nectarine

1 apricot

6 ounces light apricot yogurt, frozen

1/2 cup sugar-free lemonade

Directions

Combine all ingredients in a blender and purée until smooth.

Pour into two chilled glasses.

Kale Mango Smoothie with Tangerine

(Ready in about 15 minutes | Servings 2)

Ingredients

1¼ cups chopped kale leaves, stems removed

1¼ cups mango, diced

2 medium ribs celery, chopped

1 cup fresh tangerine, cut into sections

1/4 cup chopped fresh parsley

1 tablespoon sunflower seeds

Directions

Place all ingredients in a blender.

Pulse until all ingredients are well incorporated.

Pour the prepared smoothie into 2 chilled glasses.

Power Energy Fruit Smoothie

(Ready in about 10 minutes | Servings 2)

Ingredients

1/2 banana

1/2 cup blueberries

1/4 ripe avocado

1/2 cup almond milk

1 scoop vanilla protein powder

Directions

Combine all ingredients in your blender and purée until smooth and frothy.

Pour into prepared glasses and add ice cubes (optional).

Orange Apricot Yogurt Smoothie

(Ready in about 10 minutes | Servings 1)

Ingredients

1/4 cup orange juice

1/2 cup plain yogurt

1/2 cup fresh apricots, peeled and pitted

1 teaspoon raw honey

Directions

Place all ingredients in a blender.

Blend on high speed until smooth. Serve in tall chilled glass.

Papaya Coconut Smoothie

(Ready in about 10 minutes | Servings 2)

Ingredients

1 cup papaya

1 cup coconut yogurt

Juice from 1/2 fresh lemon

1 tablespoon honey of choice

Directions

Cut the papaya into the chunks and place them in a blender jar. Add coconut yogurt, lemon juice and honey.

Blend until smoothie consistency is reached.

Pour into tall glasses and serve immediately.

Banana Vanilla Shake

(Ready in about 10 minutes | Servings 4)

Ingredients

1/2 cup plain yogurt

1/2 cup skim milk

1 banana

1/8 teaspoon cinnamon

1/8 teaspoon grated nutmeg

1/2 teaspoon vanilla extract

8 ice cubes

Directions

In a blender, place all ingredients and blend to desired consistency.

Serve immediately.

Sweet Potato and Pumpkin Smoothie

(Ready in about 15 minutes | Servings 2)

Ingredients

1 sweet potato

1 carrot, quartered

1/2 cup pumpkin

1/4 avocado, pitted and peeled

1/2 cup milk

1/8 teaspoon cinnamon

1/8 teaspoon cardamom

Directions

Cut the sweet potato into small chunks.

In your blender, place sweet potatoes and carrots first.

Then add the rest of ingredients and pulse until a smooth consistency develops.

Serve at room temperature or chilled. Top with whip cream and pecans (optional).

Strawberry Cucumber Smoothie

(Ready in about 10 minutes | Servings 1)

Ingredients

6 strawberries

1 banana, peeled

Seeds from 1 pomegranate

1/8 teaspoon grated nutmeg

1/4 teaspoon ground cloves

1 cucumber, quartered

Directions

Add all ingredients to the blender and blend until the mixture is thickened.

If needed, add a little water and blend again. Serve at once.

Tropical Charm Smoothie

(Ready in about 10 minutes | Servings 2)

Ingredients

1 guava, peeled

1/4 cantaloupe, peeled and seeded

1 carrot with greens

1/2 cup non- dairy milk

Directions

Simply blend all four ingredients together.

Pour into 3 chilled glasses.

Plum Watermelon Smoothie

(Ready in about 5 minutes | Servings 1)

Ingredients

2 plums, pitted

1 cup watermelon, cubed

1 small cucumber, quartered

Directions

In your blender, place the plums and watermelon. Add 1 small cucumber, it can reduce the sweetness.

Purée the ingredients and add ice cubes if you like it. Drink immediately.

Avocado Mango Smoothie

(Ready in about 5 minutes | Servings 1)

Ingredients

1 avocado, pitted and peeled

1 mango, pitted and peeled

1/8 teaspoon cilantro

1/2 lemon, peeled

1/2 cup strawberries, capped

1/4 cup water

Directions

Add all ingredients to the blender or a food processor and purée until the mixture reaches the desired consistency.

Serve immediately poured into tall glass and garnished with fruit slices.

Hangover Vegetable Smoothie

(Ready in about 10 minutes | Servings 2)

Ingredients

1 cup cauliflower florets

1 cup broccoli florets

1 apple, cored and quartered

1 orange, peeled

Directions

Blend the cauliflower and broccoli first. Then add the fruits and blend until nice and smooth.

Drink immediately. This refreshing smoothie relieves the effects of alcohol consumption and hangover.

Refreshing Pear Apple Smoothie

(Ready in about 10 minutes | Servings 3)

Ingredients

1 pear, cored and quartered

1 Granny Smith apple, cored and quartered

1 carrot with greens

2 kiwis, peeled

4 sprigs mint

Directions

Blend all ingredients until your smoothie reaches the desired consistency.

Serve immediately, poured into tall glasses and garnished with pear slices.

Sweet Potato Maple Smoothie

(Ready in about 10 minutes | Servings 2)

Ingredients

1/2 cup sweet potato

1/2 cup plain yogurt

1 cup milk

1 tablespoon maple syrup

1/4 teaspoon Allspice

2 tablespoon whip cream

1 teaspoon chopped almonds

Directions

To cook the sweet potatoes: using a fork, make several poke holes in the sweet potato.

Wrap the potato in a damp paper towel, and microwave until it is fork tender. Allow the potato to cool and peel off the skin.

In a blender, combine potato with yogurt, milk, maple syrup, and Allspice.

Purée until the mixture is smooth and thick. Pour into a glass and top with whip cream and almonds.

Grape Guava Shake

(Ready in about 5 minutes | Servings 2)

Ingredients

1 cup grapes of choice

1 cup watermelon

1 cup raspberries

1 guava, peeled

1/2 cup coconut milk

Coconut flakes for garnish

Directions

In a blender, process grapes, watermelon, raspberries, guava and coconut milk until nice and smooth.

Pour into the glasses and sprinkle the coconut over the top.

Fruit Mint Smoothie

(Ready in about 5 minutes | Servings 2)

Ingredients

1 cup cherries, pitted

4 sprigs mint

1/2 small cucumber, quartered

1 cup raspberries

1 apple, cored and quartered

1/2 cup coconut water

Directions

In a blender, combine ingredients and purée until the mixture develops the desired consistency.

Serve immediately, poured into tall glasses and garnished with cherries.

Detox Vegetable Juice

(Ready in about 5 minutes | Servings 4)

Ingredients

6 carrots

3 large tomatoes

2 green bell peppers

2 cloves garlic

4 stalks celery

1 cup watercress

1 cup loosely packed spinach

Directions

Blend all ingredients until smooth.

Drink immediately.

Exotic Mango Breakfast

(Ready in about 5 minutes | Servings 2)

Ingredients

1/2 mango, pitted and peeled

3 sprigs mint

1 cup pomegranate seeds

1/4 papaya, seeded and peeled

1/2 cup almond milk

Directions

Blend all five ingredients together.

Pour into two glasses and sprinkle chopped almonds on top (optional).

Vitamin Berry Lemon Smoothie

(Ready in about 5 minutes | Servings 2)

Ingredients

1 cup cherries, pitted

1 cup blueberries

1 cup raspberries

1/2 lemon, peeled

Directions

In a blender, process berries and lemon until the mixture is nice and smooth.

Pour into the glasses and enjoy.

Fizzy Cherry, Apple and Mint

(Ready in about 5 minutes | Servings 2)

Ingredients

1 apple, cored and quartered

1 cup sour cherries, pitted

2 sprigs mint

2 ounces seltzer water

Directions

Blend the apple, cherries, and mint.

Add the seltzer water to the blender, and pulse once or twice.

Pour into the glasses and serve.

Avocado Gazpacho Smoothie

(Ready in about 15 minutes | Servings 4)

Ingredients

1/2 cup water

2 cloves garlic, peeled

1 cucumber, quartered

1 avocado, pitted and peeled

1 green bell pepper, seeded

1 medium zucchini, quartered

2 scallions

Salt to taste

Directions

Add the water, garlic, cucumber, and avocado to the blender.

Pulse a few times and then add the pepper, zucchini, scallions and salt.

Blend until the mixture is smooth and thick. Pour into 4 glasses and serve.

Carrot Orange Smoothie

(Ready in about 5 minutes | Servings 1)

Ingredients

4 medium carrots

1 medium orange, peeled

1 cup kale

1/2 medium avocado

Directions

Toss all ingredients into the blender. Cover and blend till nice and smooth.

Pour into a glass and drink.

Asparagus Vitality Smoothie

(Ready in about 10 minutes | Servings 2)

Ingredients

4 stalks asparagus tips, tender halves only

1 apple, cored and quartered

1/2 cup water

2 cups romaine lettuce, chopped

1 cup grapes

Directions

Add the asparagus, apple, and water to the blender, and process until the ingredients are broken into small chunks.

Then add remaining ingredients and purée until the mixture becomes smooth and thick.

Pour into two glasses and enjoy.

Pre-workout Snack Smoothie

(Ready in about 5 minutes | Servings 2)

Ingredients

1 cup green grapes

2 kiwis, peeled

1 banana, peeled

Directions

In a blender, process all ingredients until a smooth consistency develops.

Pour into two chilled glasses and drink. If you feel it's needed, you can add a water.

Tropical Breakfast Smoothie

(Ready in about 5 minutes | Servings 2)

Ingredients

1/4 medium pineapple, peeled

1/4 cantaloupe, peeled and seeded

1 cup spinach

1 orange, peeled

1 cup pomegranate seeds

Directions

Combine all five ingredients in your blender.

Cover and blend till the smoothie reaches your desired consistency.

Pour into two chilled glasses and enjoy this smoothie which is an excellent breakfast for your brain.

Carrot Coconut Smoothie

(Ready in about 10 minutes | Servings 2)

Ingredients

1 yellow beet

1 carrot with greens

1 orange, peeled

1/2 cup coconut water

Directions

In your blender, process the beet and the carrot.

Then add the orange and coconut water and pulse a few times until the mixture reaches the desired consistency.

Pour into glasses and sprinkle coconut flakes on top (optional).

Enjoy this excellent smoothie as a source of beta-carotene and anti-oxidants.

Potato Pineapple Smoothie

(Ready in about 10 minutes | Servings 2)

Ingredients

1 red potato, cooked

1/4 inch ginger slice

1/4 pineapple, peeled and chopped

2 kiwis, peeled

A dash of grated nutmeg

Directions

Process the potato and ginger in a blender.

Then add the pineapple and kiwi and pulse a few times until the mixture is thick and smooth.

Pour into glasses. This super healthy drink is good for your digestion.

Cranberry Lemonade Smoothie

(Ready in about 10 minutes | Servings 4)

Ingredients

1 cup cranberries

2 lemons, peeled

3 cups water

Directions

In a blender container, combine ingredients and purée until the smoothie develops the desired consistency.

Pour into four glasses.

This smoothie is a high-quality drink for your kidneys.

Banana Coffee Shake

(Ready in about 10 minutes | Servings 2)

Ingredients

2 frozen bananas, peeled

1 ½ cups skim milk

1 cup low-fat coffee yogurt

1/4 teaspoon ground cinnamon

1/8 teaspoon ground cloves

1/8 teaspoon ground nutmeg

Fresh mint leaves for garnish

Directions

In your blender, combine frozen bananas, milk, yogurt, cinnamon, cloves and nutmeg.

Cover and blend until nice and smooth. Garnish with fresh mint leaves and serve in chilled glasses.

Banana Vanilla Shake

(Ready in about 10 minutes | Servings 3)

Ingredients

1 banana, sliced

1/2 cup yogurt

2 cups milk

2 teaspoons pure vanilla essence

Directions

Put banana, yogurt, 1/2 cup of milk and vanilla essence into a blender. Process till the banana is mashed.

Add remaining milk and blend until smoothie consistency is reached.

Pour into chilled glasses and drink immediately.

Banana Strawberry Shake

(Ready in about 5 minutes | Servings 2)

Ingredients

2 frozen bananas

1 cup frozen or fresh strawberries

1 cup vanilla rice milk

1 teaspoon vanilla extract

2 tablespoons maple syrup

1/8 teaspoon grated nutmeg

1/8 teaspoon cinnamon

Directions

In a blender container, combine ingredients and purée till your smoothie develops the desired consistency.

Pour into glasses and serve immediately.

Apple Berry Smoothie

(Ready in about 5 minutes | Servings 4)

Ingredients

1 cup apple juice

1 1/2 cups lemonade

1 cup frozen raspberries

1/2 cup frozen strawberries

1 cup raspberry sherbet

Directions

Add all liquid ingredients to the blender. Then add all frozen ingredients.

Blend at mix setting for 30 seconds, then blend at smooth setting. Blend until smooth and frothy.

Pour into prepared glasses and drink immediately.

Berry Blast Smoothie

(Ready in about 5 minutes | Servings 1)

Ingredients

1/2 cup frozen strawberries

1/2 cup frozen blueberries

1/2 cup frozen raspberries

1/2 cup apple juice

1/2 cup nonfat frozen yogurt

1/2 cup ice

Directions

Combine ingredients in a blender or a food processor and mix until smooth.

Pour into chilled glass and enjoy!

Peachy Red Smoothie

(Ready in about 5 minutes | Servings 2)

Ingredients

1/2 cup apple juice

1/2 cup nonfat vanilla yogurt

1 cup fresh peaches, pitted

1/2 cup frozen raspberries

1 ½ cups ice chips

Directions

Combine ingredients in a blender and mix until smooth.

Pour into two glasses and serve.

Berry Vitality Smoothie

(Ready in about 5 minutes | Servings 1)

Ingredients

1/4 cup blueberries

1/4 cup blackberries

1 banana

1/2 cup apple juice

1/3 cup raspberry sorbet

Directions

Put all ingredients into your blender.

Mix until smooth and frothy.

Black Cherry Smoothie

(Ready in about 5 minutes | Servings 1)

Ingredients

1/2 cup yogurt

1/2 cup frozen black cherries

1 teaspoon honey

1/2 teaspoon vanilla extract

Directions

Place ingredients in your blender or a food processor, cover and purée until smoothie consistency is reached.

Transfer to the glass, garnish with cherries and drink immediately.

Apricot Orange Smoothie

(Ready in about 5 minutes | Servings 2)

Ingredients

1 cup vanilla yogurt

1 cup apricots, pitted

1/4 cup wheat germ

1/2 cup orange juice

1/2 cup ice cubes

Directions

Add all ingredients to the blender or a food processor and mix until the smoothie reaches the desired consistency.

Pour into tall glasses, garnish with orange wedges and drink immediately.

Chocolate Peanut Butter Smoothie

(Ready in about 5 minutes | Servings 2)

Ingredients

1/2 cup soy milk

1/2 cup silken tofu

1/3 cup creamy peanut butter

2 frozen bananas

2 tablespoons chocolate syrup

4 ice cubes

Directions

Combine soy milk, tofu, and peanut butter in a blender or a food processor.

Add bananas, chocolate syrup, ice cubes.

Mix until smooth and thick.

Pear Ginger Smoothie

(Ready in about 5 minutes | Servings 1)

Ingredients

1 ½ cup pears, diced

1/2 cup yogurt

1/2 cup pear nectar

1 teaspoon lemon juice

1/4 teaspoon fresh ginger, grated

1/2 teaspoon vanilla extract

4 ice cubes

A dash of ground cinnamon

Directions

Toss all ingredients into a blender or a food processor.

Cover and blend until thick and smooth.

Pour into a tall glass. Sprinkle the cinnamon on top and drink.

Pear Walnut Smoothie

(Ready in about 5 minutes | Servings 2)

Ingredients

1 ripe pear, peeled and quartered

3 tablespoons lemon juice

1/4 cup walnut kernels, chopped

1 cup buttermilk

1 tablespoon honey

Directions

Combine all ingredients and purée with an electric blender or a food processor.

Transfer to the tall glasses and serve.

Pina Colada Smoothie

(Ready in about 10 minutes | Servings 4)

Ingredients

5 tablespoons coconut milk

2 ½ cups pineapple juice

1/2 cup vanilla ice cream

1/2 frozen banana, quartered

1 ½ cups frozen pineapple chunks

Directions

Pour all liquid ingredients into your blender first. Then add all frozen ingredients.

Blend at mix setting for 30 seconds, then blend at smooth setting.

Pour into the tall glasses and drink immediately.

Cocoa Pina Colada Smoothie

(Ready in about 5 minutes | Servings 1)

Ingredients

1 cup frozen pineapple chunks

1 tablespoon coconut flakes

1 teaspoon raw cocoa powder

1/2 cup coconut water

1/2 cup almond milk

Directions

Put all ingredients into your blender.

Mix well until smoothie consistency is reached.

Pour into chilled glass and serve.

Mango Pina Colada Smoothie

(Ready in about 10 minutes | Servings 4)

Ingredients

1 mango, peeled and seeded

2 tablespoons maple syrup

1 ¼ cups pineapple juice

1/2 cup heavy cream

1 (14-ounce) can coconut milk

1 ¼ cups ice cubes

Directions

Combine all ingredients and purée with an electric blender or a food processor.

Pour into four tall glasses and serve chilled.

Pineapple Buttermilk Smoothie

(Ready in about 10 minutes | Servings 3)

Ingredients

20 ounces unsweetened pineapple chunks

1 cup buttermilk

1 tablespoon vanilla extract

1 tablespoon honey

Mint leaves for garnish (optional)

Directions

Drain pineapple. Reserve 1/2 cup of juice and freeze the pineapple chunks.

Place pineapple juice, buttermilk, vanilla, honey and frozen pineapple into a blender or a food processor. Mix until smooth and thick.

Transfer to the glasses and garnish with mint if desired.

Pineapple Berry Smoothie

(Ready in about 10 minutes | Servings 2)

Ingredients

1 cup orange juice

1/4 cup pineapple juice

2 pineapple rings

6 fresh or frozen strawberries

13-14 frozen raspberries

13-14 frozen blueberries

1 teaspoon vanilla extract

3 ounces yogurt

Ice cubes to taste

Directions

Put all ingredients into an electric blender or a food processor.

Process until the smoothie consistency is reached.

Pour into glasses and drink immediately.

Spinach Strawberry Smoothie

(Ready in about 10 minutes | Servings 4)

Ingredients

2 cups frozen spinach

2 cups frozen strawberries

1 frozen banana

2 tablespoons maple syrup

1/2 cup ice

Directions

Place all ingredients into your blender, cover and purée until smoothie consistency is reached.

Transfer to the glass, garnish with strawberries and enjoy!

Spiced Pumpkin Smoothie

(Ready in about 5 minutes | Servings 4)

Ingredients

2 cups pumpkin puree

2 cups milk

1/4 cup brown sugar

1 teaspoon ground cinnamon

1/2 teaspoon vanilla extract

1/2 teaspoon grated nutmeg

Directions

Combine all ingredients in your blender.

Blend well until smoothie consistency is reached.

Transfer to the tall glasses and serve. Dust with a little cinnamon powder (optional).

Yam Banana Smoothie

(Ready in about 15 minutes | Servings 4)

Ingredients

1 medium yam

1 ½ cups vanilla yogurt

1/2 cup milk

1 cup ice cubes

1 teaspoon sugar

1 ripe frozen banana

Directions

Prick the yam with a fork. Microwave the yam for 8 to 10 minutes, until fork tender.

Allow it to cool, and then peel the yam.

Combine the yam with remaining ingredients in the container of a blender. Blend until smooth.

Zucchini Orange Smoothie

(Ready in about 5 minutes | Servings 3)

Ingredients

1 zucchini, cubed

5 ice cubes

1 cup orange juice

2 tablespoons sucralose sweetener

3/4 teaspoon vanilla extract

Directions

Place all five ingredients into your blender.

Cover, and mix until the smoothie reaches the desired consistency.

Serve in the tall glasses.

Cocoa Zucchini Shake

(Ready in about 10 minutes | Servings 4)

Ingredients

1 cup frozen zucchini, grated

2 large frozen bananas, peeled

2 tablespoons cocoa powder

1/4 cup peanuts, chopped

1/2 cup sugar

1 cup half-and-half

Directions

Place all of the ingredients into your blender or a food processor.

Cover, and mix until the smoothie reaches the desired consistency.

Serve immediately.

Cantaloupe Yogurt Smoothie

(Ready in about 10 minutes | Servings 1)

Ingredients

1 ripe frozen banana, partially thawed and cut into chunks

1/4 ripe cantaloupe, seeded and cut into chunks

1/2 cup low-fat yogurt

2 tablespoons skim milk powder

1 tablespoon orange juice

Honey to taste (optional)

Directions

Combine all ingredients in a blender and process until smooth and uniform.

Pour into a chilled and a tall glass and drink immediately.

Cantaloupe Raspberries Smoothie

(Ready in about 5 minutes | Servings 2)

Ingredients

1/2 cantaloupe, peeled, seeded and cut into chunks

1/2 cup plain yogurt

1 cup raspberries

2 tablespoons maple syrup

Directions

In a blender, combine all four ingredients.

Mix until a smooth consistency develops.

Pour into two glasses and serve.

Cherry Cantaloupe Smoothie

(Ready in about 5 minutes | Servings 1)

Ingredients

1/2 cantaloupe, peeled, seeded, and sliced

1/2 cup apricot juice

3-4 pitted cherries

1/4 cup blackberries

3-4 ice cubes

Directions

Put all five ingredients into a blender.

Blend until smoothie consistency is reached.

Pour into a glass and serve.

Carrot Apple Smoothie

(Ready in about 5 minutes | Servings 2)

Ingredients

2 cups carrot juice

1/2 cup apple juice

6 ounces plain yogurt, frozen

1 banana

Directions

In a blender or a food processor, process all ingredients until the mixture is nice and smooth.

Pour into the glasses and enjoy.

Vegan Vanilla Cherry Smoothie

(Ready in about 5 minutes | Servings 1)

Ingredients

1/4 cup cherry sugar-free syrup

1/4 cup vanilla sugar-free syrup

2 scoops Vege Fuel

1 ½ cups crushed ice

Directions

Purée all ingredients in a blender until smooth and uniform.

Pour into a chilled tall glass and enjoy.

Chocolate Banana Smoothie

(Ready in about 5 minutes | Servings 1)

Ingredients

1 frozen banana -- peeled

6 ounces light frozen cherry yogurt

2 tablespoons chocolate syrup

1/2 cup non-fat milk

Directions

Combine all four ingredients and purée with an electric blender or a food processor.

Transfer to a glass and drink immediately.

Chocolate Dream Smoothie

(Ready in about 5 minutes | Servings 2)

Ingredients

1 milk chocolate bar

2 scoops chocolate ice cream

1/2 cup milk

Ice cubes to taste

Directions

In a blender, process milk chocolate bar first.

Add ice cream, milk and ice cubes and pulse until the mixture is creamy, nice and smooth.

Blueberry Yogurt Smoothie

(Ready in about 5 minutes | Servings 2)

Ingredients

6 ounces frozen fat-free blueberry yogurt

1 cup blueberries, fresh

1 cup nonfat milk

Directions

Combine all three ingredients and purée in order to make a mixture smooth and creamy.

Transfer to the chilled glasses and serve.

Cantaloupe Vanilla Yogurt Smoothie

(Ready in about 5 minutes | Servings 2)

Ingredients

1/2 ripe cantaloupe, peeled, seeded, and cut into chunks

1 cup milk

1 cup vanilla fat-free yogurt

1 cup crushed ice

2 tablespoons sugar

Ground cinnamon to taste

Ground nutmeg to taste

Ground cloves to taste

Directions

Combine all ingredients in a blender and purée to the consistency you prefer.

Pour into glasses and serve.

Anti-aging Smoothie

(Ready in about 10 minutes | Servings 2)

Ingredients

1/2 cup water

1 plum, pitted

2 kiwis, peeled

2 cups spinach

1 teaspoon ginger, grated

Fresh mint leaves for garnish

Directions

Add the water, plum, and kiwis to the blender first. Pulse for a few seconds.

Add the spinach and ginger, and pulse until the mixture is thick and smooth.

Garnish with the mint leaves and serve in the tall glasses.

Multivitamin Smoothie

(Ready in about 10 minutes | Servings 3)

Ingredients

1 cup carrot, thinly sliced

1 banana

1 kiwi, peeled

1 apple, peeled, cored, and sliced

1 cup pineapple, peeled and cut into chunks

1 cup crushed ice

1 tablespoon chia seeds

Directions

Toss all ingredients into your blender.

Cover and blend until the mixture is nice and smooth.

Pour into the glasses and enjoy.

Italian Style Smoothie

(Ready in about 10 minutes | Servings 2)

Ingredients

1 tomato

1 clove garlic

1 green bell pepper, seeded

A few basil leaves

A dash of oregano

2 kale leaves

Directions

Place all ingredients into a blender and process until the smoothie reaches your desired consistency.

If you feel it's needed and if this smoothie is too thick, you can add a water.

Pour into the glasses and serve. You can serve this smoothie as a chilled soup, too.

Carrot Mint Smoothie

(Ready in about 10 minutes | Servings 2)

Ingredients

1 carrot with greens

1 green apple, cored and quartered

1/2 cup water

1 small cucumber, quartered

1/2 teaspoon grated ginger

8 mint leaves

Directions

Combine the carrot, apple and water in your blender. Blend on the "chop" setting.

Then add the cucumber, ginger and 4 mint leaves. Blend until smooth and uniform.

Pour into two glasses. This amazing drink naturally improves a good eyesight and digestion.

Beet Cranberry Smoothie

(Ready in about 10 minutes | Servings 2)

Ingredients

1 beet, with greens

1 cup cranberries

1 cup watermelon

1/2 cup water

Directions

In a blender or a food processor, pulse the beet first.

Then add the rest of ingredients and blend until the smoothie reaches your desired consistency.

Pour into tall chilled glasses and serve.

Rejuvenating Detox Smoothie

(Ready in about 10 minutes | Servings 3)

Ingredients

1 small sweet potato, cut into chunks

1 beet, with or without greens

1 carrot with greens

1 cucumber, quartered

1 tablespoon chia seeds

Directions

In a blender, process the sweet potato and beet first. Then add the carrot and cucumber.

Pour into the glasses and enjoy this great smoothie that fights wrinkles.

Spinach and Fruit Smoothie

(Ready in about 10 minutes | Servings 4)

Ingredients

2 cups baby spinach

2 pears, peeled, cored, and quartered

2 bananas, quartered

1 cup carrots, chopped

1 cup orange juice

1 cup fresh blueberries

1 cup crushed ice

Directions

Blend all ingredients until smooth and thick, or 1 to 2 minutes.

Pour into tall glasses and drink immediately.

Frosty Vegan Smoothie

(Ready in about 10 minutes | Servings 1)

Ingredients

1 cup soy milk

1/2 cup baby spinach

1/2 cup water

1/2 cup frozen banana, cut into chunks

1/2 cup frozen pineapple, chopped

Directions

In a blender, combine soy milk and baby spinach first. Mix until the spinach leaves are puréed.

Then add water, banana, and pineapple.

Blend until the smoothie reaches your desired consistency. Pour into a glass and drink immediately.

Energy-Boosting Smoothie

(Ready in about 10 minutes | Servings 1)

Ingredients

1 cup water

1/2 mango

1 cup baby spinach

1/3 cup baby carrots

1/2 cup cauliflower florets

1/4 cup blueberries, or to taste

1 stalk celery

1/2 orange, peeled

1 tablespoon honey

Directions

Combine all ingredients in your blender.

Blend on high speed until smooth and uniform.

Pumpkin Greek Yogurt

(Ready in about 5 minutes | Servings 1)

Ingredients

4 cubes ice

1 cup milk

1/3 cup pumpkin puree

1/3 cup Greek yogurt

1/2 frozen banana, cut into chunks

1 pinch ground cinnamon

1 pinch ground nutmeg

1 teaspoon vanilla extract

Directions

Place all ingredients in your blender.

Cover and blend until the smoothie reaches your desired consistency.

Pour into a glass and serve immediately.

Pineapple Fig Smoothie

(Ready in about 10 minutes | Servings 3)

Ingredients

1 cup fresh pineapple, chopped

8 dried figs

1 tablespoon vanilla extract

1/4 cup frozen blackberries

1/2 cup kale leaves, chopped

1 cup frozen pineapple, chopped

Directions

In a blender, mix pineapple, figs and vanilla first.

Add blackberries and mix 1 minute.

Then add the kale and frozen pineapple and blend until smooth and creamy.

Divide this smoothie among three tall glasses and enjoy!

Vegetable Berry Smoothie

(Ready in about 5 minutes | Servings 1)

Ingredients

1 cup fresh kale

1 beet, peeled and chopped

1/2 cup plain Greek yogurt

1 cup frozen blackberries

1/2 cup crushed ice

4 slices zucchini

Directions

Combine all ingredients in a blender.

Cover and purée until the mixture is smooth and frothy.

Pour into a glass and enjoy.

Vegetable Yogurt Smoothie with Oats

(Ready in about 10 minutes | Servings 1)

Ingredients

1 zucchini, peeled, grated, and chopped

1 carrot, peeled, grated, and chopped

1/2 cup Greek yogurt

1/2 cup skim milk

2 tablespoons rolled oats

2 tablespoons honey

1 tablespoon chia seeds

Directions

Toss all ingredients into the blender.

Cover and blend until creamy and smooth.

Pour into a glass and enjoy.

Sunday Family Smoothie

(Ready in about 15 minutes | Servings 6)

Ingredients

1 cup watermelon

1 cup Honeydew

1 cup pineapple

1 cup mango

1 cup strawberries

1/4 cup sugar of choice

1 cup orange juice

Crushed ice to taste

Directions

Cut the fruits into chunks. In your blender, mix all ingredients.

Cover and blend on high speed. Repeat with remaining fruit.

Garnish with fruit (optional). Divide this smoothie among six chilled glasses and drink immediately.

Easy Three-Ingredient Smoothie

(Ready in about 5 minutes | Servings 1)

Ingredients

3/4 cup pineapple juice

1 cup frozen strawberries

1 ripe frozen banana

Directions

Toss all ingredients into your blender.

Cover and blend until creamy and smooth.

Pour into a glass and drink immediately.

Mixed Fruit Yogurt Smoothie

(Ready in about 5 minutes | Servings 1)

Ingredients

1/2 cup vanilla yogurt

1/4 cup skim milk

1 frozen banana

1 cup frozen mixed berries of choice

1 tablespoon maple syrup

1/2 teaspoon vanilla extract

Directions

Place all ingredients in a blender.

Cover and blend until the smoothie reaches your desired consistency.

Pour into a glass and drink immediately.

Frozen Vanilla Yogurt Smoothie

(Ready in about 5 minutes | Servings 1)

Ingredients

1 scoop frozen vanilla yogurt

1 cup apple juice, frozen

1 apple, cored and quartered

1 ripe pear, cored and quartered

Raw honey to taste

Chocolate syrup

Crushed ice (optional)

Directions

Process all of the ingredients in your blender until smooth and uniform.

Pour into a tall glass and serve.

Cinnamon Fruit Smoothie

(Ready in about 10 minutes | Servings 4)

Ingredients

1 peach

3/4 cup fresh strawberries

1/2 banana

2 cups chilled milk

2 tablespoons frozen orange juice concentrate

4-6 ice cubes

1 teaspoon ground cinnamon

1/2 teaspoon grated nutmeg

Directions

Combine fruit, milk and orange juice in a blender.

Then add ice cubes one at a time.

Pour into the glasses, sprinkle with the cinnamon on top and serve.

Fruit Cocktail Smoothie

(Ready in about 10 minutes | Servings 4)

Ingredients

1 cup Fruit cocktail, chilled

1 cup skim milk

1/4 cup nonfat dry milk powder

1/2 teaspoon almond extract

1/2 cup ice cubes

Chopped almonds for garnish (optional)

Directions

In a blender, place fruit cocktail with milk, milk powder and almond extract.

Cover and mix until all ingredients are well combined.

Add ice cubes, cover and blend until smooth and creamy.

Divide among four chilled glasses, sprinkle almonds on top (optional) and serve.

Lemony Melon Smoothie with Grapes

(Ready in about 10 minutes | Servings 2)

Ingredients

1 ½ cups honeydew melon, cut into chunks

1/2 cup nonfat lemon yogurt

1 cup frozen grapes

1 tablespoon chopped fresh mint

1 tablespoon lemon juice

Directions

Toss all of the ingredients into your blender.

Cover and blend until uniform, creamy and smooth.

Transfer to the chilled glasses and enjoy!

Orange-Banana Oat Smoothie

(Ready in about 5 minutes | Servings 2)

Ingredients

1 medium orange, peeled and sliced

1 ripe banana

2 tablespoons rolled oats

2 cups rice milk

Directions

Combine all of the ingredients in a blender container.

Cover tightly with the lid and blend until smooth.

Transfer to the chilled glasses and enjoy!

Banana Cereal Smoothie

(Ready in about 5 minutes | Servings 2)

Ingredients

1 ripe banana, peeled

2 tablespoons granola

2 tablespoons wheat germ

2 cups milk

1/2 teaspoon Allspice

1 teaspoon chia seeds

Directions

Purée all ingredients in a blender until smooth, or 1 to 2 minutes.

Divide among two chilled glasses and serve.

Fruit Almond Smoothie

(Ready in about 5 minutes | Servings 2)

Ingredients

2 medium plums, sliced

1 cup frozen strawberries, halved

2 cups almond milk

Chopped almonds for garnish (optional)

Directions

Combine all of the ingredients in an electric blender or a food processor.

Blend until smoothie consistency is reached.

Transfer to the tall glasses, scatter almonds on top and serve.

Berry Vitality Smoothie

(Ready in about 5 minutes | Servings 2)

Ingredients

1 ½ cups boysenberry flavor juice

1/2 cup boysenberries

1/2 cup blackberries

1 cup blueberries, frozen

1 tablespoon sunflower seeds

Directions

Place all four ingredients in a blender container. Put lid on tightly.

Pulse until smoothie consistency is reached.

Serve in chilled tall glasses.

Fruit Energy Smoothie

(Ready in about 5 minutes | Servings 1)

Ingredients

1/2 cup orange juice

1 banana

6-7 frozen strawberries

4 frozen peaches, peeled and sliced

5-6 frozen blackberries

1/8 teaspoon nutmeg

1 teaspoon raw honey

6 ice cubes

Fresh mint leaves for garnish

Directions

Put orange juice, banana, strawberries, peaches, blackberries, nutmeg and honey in your blender.

Blend until smooth, thick and creamy. Add ice, and pulse again.

Pour into a glass and garnish with some fresh mint.

Lemon Yogurt Smoothie

(Ready in about 5 minutes | Servings 1)

Ingredients

1 cup nonfat lemon yogurt

1/2 cup pineapple juice

1 ½ cup strawberries

1/2 cup crushed ice

Directions

Combine all four ingredients in your blender.

Blend until smooth, thick and creamy.

Pour into chilled glass and drink immediately.

Lime Melon Smoothie

(Ready in about 5 minutes | Servings 4)

Ingredients

1 ½ cups watermelon, cubed

1 ½ cups honeydew melon, cubed

Juice of 2 fresh limes

1 cup yogurt

1 teaspoon vanilla extract

1 cup ice cubes

Directions

Place all ingredients in a blender.

Mix until smoothie consistency is reached.

Pour into glasses and enjoy.

Mint-Melon Mango Smoothie

(Ready in about 5 minutes | Servings 2)

Ingredients

2 cups cantaloupe

1 cup honeydew melon

1 cup watermelon, seedless

1/2 cup mango juice

2 teaspoons honey

10 fresh mint leaves

3 ice cubes

Directions

Cut the fruits into chunks and place them in a blender container.

Blend until smooth.

Pour into two chilled glasses. Enjoy!

Pineapple Yogurt with Flax seeds

(Ready in about 5 minutes | Servings 2)

Ingredients

1 cup pineapple, cubed

1 cup almond milk

1 cup Greek yogurt

1 tablespoons flax seeds

1/2 cup ice cubes

Directions

In your blender, place pineapple, almond milk, Greek yogurt, and flax seeds.

Blend until smooth and thick. Add ice and pulse again.

Pour into a glass and serve.

Fruit Smoothie with Sunflower Seeds

(Ready in about 5 minutes | Servings 2)

Ingredients

1 medium peach, sliced

1/2 cup berries of choice

1 cup yogurt

1 cup skim milk

1 tablespoon sunflower seeds

Directions

Place all ingredients in your blender.

Cover and blend until smooth and creamy.

Divide your smoothie among two chilled glasses.

Exotic Papaya Shake

(Ready in about 5 minutes | Servings 2)

Ingredients

1 cup papaya, peeled and seeded

1/2 ripe banana, peeled

1/2 cup mango, cubed

2 tablespoons coconut milk

2 cups coconut water

Directions

Coarsely chop papaya.

Combine papaya with remaining ingredients in a blender. Mix until smooth.

Pour into two glasses. Top each smoothie with a dollop of whipped cream, if desired.

Papaya Orange Smoothie

(Ready in about 5 minutes | Servings 2)

Ingredients

2 ripe papayas, peeled and cut into chunks

1/2 cup fresh orange juice

1/2 cup vanilla frozen yogurt

1 tablespoons flax seeds

Directions

Place all ingredients in a blender.

Mix until smoothie consistency is reached.

Pour into two chilled glasses and enjoy.

Nectarine Papaya Smoothie

(Ready in about 5 minutes | Servings 2)

Ingredients

1 cup sugar-free lemonade

6 ounces frozen vanilla yogurt

1 nectarine, pitted

1 cup papaya, peeled and seeded

Directions

Put all four ingredients into your blender.

Mix well until smoothie consistency is reached.

Pour into glasses and serve.

Easy Red Currant Smoothie

(Ready in about 5 minutes | Servings 2)

Ingredients

1 medium orange, cut into segments

1/2 cup red currants

1/2 cup raspberries

2 cups milk of choice

1/2 teaspoon vanilla extract

Directions

Place all ingredients in a blender.

Blend until smooth and thick.

Pour into two chilled glasses and enjoy!

Peach Banana Smoothie

(Ready in about 10 minutes | Servings 5)

Ingredients

2 cups peach nectar

1 cup frozen yogurt

1 cup peach yogurt

1/2 frozen banana

1 ½ cups frozen peaches, chopped

Chocolate syrup (optional)

Directions

Pour peach nectar, yogurt and peach yogurt into a blender. Then add banana and peaches.

Blend at mix setting for 30 seconds then blend at smooth setting until smooth.

Divide among glasses and drizzle with chocolate syrup (optional).

Peach and Almond with Berries

(Ready in about 10 minutes | Servings 2)

Ingredients

1 peach, frozen

10 blueberries, frozen

1 cup light vanilla yogurt, frozen

1/2 cup skim milk

1/2 teaspoon crushed almonds

1/4 teaspoon almond extract

Agave syrup to taste

Directions

Place all of the ingredients in your blender. Mix until smooth and creamy.

Pour into glasses and top with additional toasted almonds, if desired.

Pear Ginger Smoothie

(Ready in about 5 minutes | Servings 2)

Ingredients

1 ½ cup pears, cored and diced

1/2 cup yogurt

1/2 cup pear nectar

1 tablespoon orange juice

1/4 teaspoon grated fresh ginger

Directions

Place the ingredients in a blender and process on high until smooth.

Pour into two glasses and garnish with pear slices, if desired.

Pumpkin Coconut Smoothie

(Ready in about 10 minutes | Servings 2)

Ingredients

1 cup pumpkin puree

2/3 cup coconut milk

2 tablespoons almond butter

1/2 frozen banana

2 dried dates, pitted

Coconut flakes for garnish

Directions

Place all ingredients in a blender.

Mix well until smoothie consistency is reached.

Pour into glasses, sprinkle with coconut flakes and serve.

Pistachio Banana Smoothie

(Ready in about 10 minutes | Servings 2)

Ingredients

1 cup nonfat yogurt

2-3 ounces pistachio instant pudding mix

2 small ripe banana

1/2 cup skim milk

Directions

Place all of the ingredients in a blender. Process until smooth and creamy.

Pour into glasses and top with chopped pistachios, if desired.

Strawberry Smoothie with Oats

(Ready in about 5 minutes | Servings 1)

Ingredients

1 cup strawberry juice

1 cup frozen strawberries

1 cup yogurt

2/3 cup oats

1/2 cup ice cubes

Directions

Place strawberry juice, strawberries, yogurt and oats in a blender.

Blend on high for 2 minutes. Gradually add ice cubes and blend until smooth.

Pour into chilled glass. Enjoy!

Greek Yogurt Orange Smoothie

(Ready in about 5 minutes | Servings 4)

Ingredients

4 cups ice

4 cups orange juice

12 ounces Greek Yogurt

1 teaspoon vanilla extract

Agave nectar to taste

Whipped cream for garnish

Directions

In a blender, place first five ingredients.

Mix until creamy and smooth.

Pour into glasses and top with whipped cream

Refreshing Chocolate Peppermint

(Ready in about 5 minutes | Servings 4)

Ingredients

1½ cups unsweetened almond milk

1/2 ripe large banana

2 tablespoons unsweetened cocoa powder

1 tablespoon peppermint extract

1 cup baby spinach

1 tablespoon chia seeds

2 cups ice

Fresh mint for garnish (optional)

Directions

Place all of the ingredients (except mint leaves) in a blender.

Mix until smooth and uniform.

Pour into glasses and garnish with fresh mint leaves, if desired.

Mango Cashew Smoothie

(Ready in about 5 minutes | Servings 2)

Ingredients

1 cup mango, sliced

2 tablespoons cashew nuts

1/2 teaspoon fresh grated ginger

1½ cup milk

1 teaspoon chia seeds

Directions

Put all ingredients into your blender.

Mix well until smoothie consistency is reached.

Pour into two chilled glasses. Enjoy!

Fruit Ice Cream Smoothie

(Ready in about 5 minutes | Servings 3)

Ingredients

1 cup vanilla ice cream

1 cup frozen blueberries

1/2 cup peaches, sliced

1/2 cup pineapple juice

1/4 cup yogurt

Directions

Place all of the ingredients in a blender container. Put lid on tightly.

Pulse until smoothie consistency is reached.

Serve in chilled tall glasses.

Fruit Vanilla Ice Cream Smoothie

(Ready in about 10 minutes | Servings 2)

Ingredients

1 cup fresh strawberries

1 frozen banana, sliced

1 cup peaches, pitted and sliced

1 cup apples

1 ½ cups vanilla ice cream

1 ½ cups ice cubes

1/2 cup milk

Directions

Put all ingredients into a smoothie mixer.

Blend until smoothie consistency is reached.

Pour into two chilled glass. Enjoy.

Sweet Potato with Almond and Dates

(Ready in about 5 minutes | Servings 1)

Ingredients

1/2 cup sweet potato, peeled, cooked and mashed

1/2 large frozen banana

2 dates, pitted

1 cup almond milk

1/4 cup water

2-3 ice cubes

Directions

Combine all ingredients in your blender and purée until smooth and uniform.

Pour into chilled glass. Sprinkle coconut flakes on top, if desired. Enjoy!

Teatime Berry Smoothie

(Ready in about 10 minutes | Servings 4)

Ingredients

2 cups unsweetened iced tea of choice

2 cups frozen mixed berries

1 cup fat-free strawberry Ice cream

Agave syrup to taste (optional)

Directions

Simply blend all of the ingredients together. Add agave syrup, if desired.

Pour into chilled glasses. Enjoy!

Easy Chocolate Banana Smoothie

(Ready in about 5 minutes | Servings 3)

Ingredients

1 large banana, frozen

2 cups low-fat chocolate milk

2/3 cup chocolate ice cream

Whipped cream for garnish (optional)

Directions

In a blender, process banana, chocolate milk and ice cream. Blend until uniform and smooth.

Pour into chilled glasses and top with whipped cream, if desired.

Antioxidant Rich Smoothie

(Ready in about 5 minutes | Servings 2)

Ingredients

1 cup blueberries

1 cup raspberries

1 cup strawberries, capped

1 cup pomegranate seeds

1/2 cup plain yogurt

Directions

In a blender, combine all of the ingredients and purée until the mixture develops the desired consistency.

Serve immediately, poured into chilled glasses and garnished with berries.

Detox Fruit Mint Smoothie

(Ready in about 5 minutes | Servings 2)

Ingredients

1/2 sweet potato

1/2 cup raspberries

1/2 cup orange, peeled

4 strawberries, capped

1/2 cucumber, quartered

4 mint sprigs

Directions

In a blender, combine ingredients and process until the smoothie develops your desired consistency.

Serve poured into chilled glasses and garnished with some extra mint leaves if desired.

Anti-Aging Vegetable Smoothie

(Ready in about 5 minutes | Servings 3)

Ingredients

1/4 head cabbage

4 kale leaves

1 beet

1 carrot

1 stalk celery

1 cup water

1 tablespoon sunflower seeds

1/4 teaspoon paprika

Fine sea salt to taste

Directions

Add the ingredients to your blender. Blend until smooth and frothy.

Pour into three glasses. Top with some extra sprouts, if desired.

Spiced Apple Vegetable Smoothie

(Ready in about 5 minutes | Servings 2)

Ingredients

1 apple, cored and quartered

1 cup pumpkin chunks

1 small cucumber, quartered

1 carrot

1/2 teaspoon ground cloves

1/2 teaspoon ground cinnamon

1/2 teaspoon grated nutmeg

1 tablespoon flax seeds

Directions

Toss all of the ingredients into your blender. Cover and blend until uniform and smooth.

Pour into two glasses and sprinkle the cinnamon on top, if desired.

Salsa Vegetable Smoothie

(Ready in about 5 minutes | Servings 3)

Ingredients

1 tomato

1 cucumber, quartered

1 jalapeño pepper, de-stemmed

2 cloves garlic

1/2 lime, peeled

3 medium sprigs cilantro

1 green onion

2 tablespoons chives for garnish

Directions

In a blender, combine cucumber, jalapeño pepper, garlic, lime, cilantro and onion.

Process the ingredients until a smooth consistency develops.

Pour into glasses and garnish with chives.

Fruit with Spinach and Cabbage

(Ready in about 5 minutes | Servings 3)

Ingredients

1 plum, seeded

1 apple, cored and quartered

2 cups baby spinach

1 cup cabbage

1/2 lemon, peeled

1 tablespoon sunflower seeds

Directions

In a blender, process all ingredients until a smooth consistency develops.

Pour into chilled glasses and enjoy!

Delicious Post-Workout Smoothie

(Ready in about 5 minutes | Servings 1)

Ingredients

1 frozen banana

1 cup yogurt

1/4 cup milk

1 teaspoon unsweetened chocolate powder

1 teaspoon honey

Directions

Combine all of the ingredients in your blender.

Cover and blend until the smoothie reaches your desired consistency.

Pour into a chilled glass. Enjoy!

Tomato Avocado Smoothie

(Ready in about 5 minutes | Servings 1)

Ingredients

1 tomato

1 avocado, pitted and peeled

1 green onion

1/2 lemon, peeled

1 tablespoon fresh parsley, chopped

1/4 cup water

Directions

In a blender container, combine ingredients and purée until the smoothie develops the desired consistency.

Divide among two glasses. This healthy smoothie can help you maintain brain health as well as fight depression.

Cantaloupe Kiwi Smoothie

(Ready in about 5 minutes | Servings 3)

Ingredients

1/4 cantaloupe, peeled and seeded

2 kiwis, peeled

1 cup raspberries

2 cups spinach

Directions

In a blender container, combine ingredients and purée until the smoothie develops the desired consistency.

Divide among three glasses. You can add a bit of water if desired.

Cleansing Cocktail Smoothie

(Ready in about 10 minutes | Servings 3)

Ingredients

5 broccoli florets

2 yellow bell peppers, de-stemmed

1/4 head green cabbage

1 handful fresh parsley

1/2 cup water

2 tomatoes

1/2 teaspoon basil leaves

Sea salt to taste

Directions

In a blender, pulse the broccoli first. Then add remaining ingredients and pulse until smooth and uniform.

Pour into the glasses and serve.

Spiced Apple Veggie Smoothie

(Ready in about 10 minutes | Servings 2)

Ingredients

1 beet with greens

1 carrot

1 apple, cored and quartered

1 inch slice ginger

1/2 cup water

1/4 teaspoon cinnamon

1/4 teaspoon ground cloves

Directions

In your blender, combine all of the ingredients.

Cover and blend until uniform and smooth.

Pour into two glasses and sprinkle the cinnamon over the top (optional).

Cold Buster Smoothie

(Ready in about 10 minutes | Servings 2)

Ingredients

1 orange, peeled

1/4 pineapple, peeled

2 carrots

1/2 teaspoon cayenne pepper

1 tablespoon lemon juice

Directions

In a blender, combine all of the ingredients.

Cover with the lid and blend until smooth.

Pour into two glasses and enjoy! This is a natural treatment of cold symptoms.

Delicious Digestive-Friendly Smoothie

(Ready in about 5 minutes | Servings 2)

Ingredients

1/2 sweet potato, cut into chunks

2 cups spinach

2 carrots

1 cup water or apple juice

Directions

Put all of the ingredients into a blender container.

Mix well until smoothie consistency is reached.

Divide among two tall chilled glasses and enjoy!

Margarita Style Smoothie

(Ready in about 10 minutes | Servings 3)

Ingredients

4 celery stalks

2 apples, cored and quartered

2 limes, peeled

1 cup water

Directions

In your blender, process the celery first.

Then blend the rest of ingredients.

Pour into three glasses and serve. Garnish with lime slices or celery, if desired.

Citrus Morning Smoothie

(Ready in about 5 minutes | Servings 2)

Ingredients

1 orange, peeled

1 lemon, peeled

1 grapefruit, peeled

Directions

In a blender container, combine ingredients and purée until your smoothie develops the desired consistency.

Pour into glasses and serve immediately.

Diabetic Energy Smoothie

(Ready in about 5 minutes | Servings 2)

Ingredients

2 stalks celery

1 tomato

1 teaspoon horseradish

1/2 lime, peeled

1/4 teaspoon cayenne pepper

Directions

In your blender, process first three ingredients.

Then add the rest of ingredients and mix until smooth and uniform.

This smoothie is a great way to normalize your blood sugar naturally.

Spiced Lemonade Smoothie

(Ready in about 5 minutes | Servings 3)

Ingredients

3 lemons, peeled

1/2 jalapeño pepper, de-stemmed

1 cucumber, quartered

2 cup water

Directions

Put all of the ingredients into a blender container.

Mix until all ingredients are well blended.

Pour into three tall glasses and serve immediately. Add ice cubes, if desired.

Cranberry Ginger with Cucumber

(Ready in about 5 minutes | Servings 2)

Ingredients

1 cup cranberries

1/2 inch slice ginger

1 cucumber, quartered

6 mint leaves

1/4 cup water

Directions

In a blender, combine all of the ingredients.

Cover with the lid and blend until smooth and uniform.

Pour into two glasses. Garnish with mint leaves (optional) and serve.

Plum and Pineapple Digestive-Friendly Smoothie

(Ready in about 5 minutes | Servings 2)

Ingredients

1/4 pineapple, peeled and cut into chunks

1 plum, seeded

5 mint leaves

1/4 head cabbage

1/4 cup water

Directions

In a blender container, combine ingredients and purée until your smoothie develops the desired consistency.

Divide among two glasses and serve immediately.

Wintertime Healthy Smoothie

(Ready in about 5 minutes | Servings 3)

Ingredients

1 sweet potato, cut into 1-inch pieces

1 cup pumpkin

1 apple, cored and quartered

1 teaspoon ground cinnamon

1/2 teaspoon grated nutmeg

1/2 teaspoon ground cloves

1 carrot

1/2 cup water

Directions

Put all ingredients into a smoothie mixer.

Blend until smoothie consistency is reached.

Divide among three glasses. Top with whipped cream (optional) and enjoy!

Fizzy Ginger Fruit Smoothie

(Ready in about 5 minutes | Servings 3)

Ingredients

2 kiwis, peeled

1 stalk celery

1 inch slice ginger

1 cucumber, quartered

1 apple, cored and quartered

1 cup cherries, pitted

1/2 cup sparkling water

Directions

Put all of the ingredients into a blender container.

Blend until all ingredients are well blended.

Pour into three glasses and garnish with slices of kiwi or apple (optional). Drink with a bendy straw and enjoy!

Fruits with Honey and Yogurt

(Ready in about 5 minutes | Servings 3)

Ingredients

1 cup yogurt

1 banana, peeled

1 mango, pitted and peeled

1 tablespoon honey

1/2 inch slice ginger

1/2 teaspoon vanilla extract

Directions

Add all ingredients to a smoothie mixer and mix until uniform and smooth.

Pour into chilled glasses and drink immediately.

Tree-Ingredient Energy Smoothie

(Ready in about 10 minutes | Servings 3)

Ingredients

1/4 pineapple, peeled

3 stalks celery

1 cucumber, quartered

Directions

Cut the pineapple into 1-inch pieces and add them to a blender container.

Add remaining ingredients and blend.

Pour into chilled glasses and enjoy!

Belly Soother Smoothie

(Ready in about 5 minutes | Servings 2)

Ingredients

1 cucumber, quartered

1 apple, cored and quartered

1 lime, peeled

1/2 bulb fennel

2 sprigs mint

1/4 inch slice ginger

Directions

In a smoothie mixer, mix all ingredients together until smooth.

Divide among glasses and enjoy!

Berry Cottage Cheese Smoothie

(Ready in about 10 minutes | Servings 4)

Ingredients

1/2 frozen banana

1/2 cup strawberries

1/4 cup blueberries

1/4 cup cottage cheese

1/2 cup almond milk

2 tablespoons maple syrup

Ice cubes to taste

Directions

Combine all of the ingredients in a blender.

Cover and blend until the smoothie reaches your desired consistency.

Divide among four chilled glasses and serve.

Orange Cottage Cheese with Almonds

(Ready in about 5 minutes | Servings 1)

Ingredients

1 orange

2 tablespoons almonds

2 tablespoons flax seeds

1 cup cottage cheese

1 scoop vanilla protein powder

1 ½ cups water

3 ice cubes

Directions

Combine all ingredients in a blender. Pulse until the mixture is smooth and creamy.

Pour into a glass and serve immediately. Add your favorite sprinkles on top and enjoy!

Vegan Morning Smoothie

(Ready in about 5 minutes | Servings 1)

Ingredients

1/2 cup plain soy yogurt

1 frozen banana

1 cup frozen black cherries

1 teaspoon raw honey

1/2 teaspoon vanilla extract

1/2 teaspoon lemon juice

Directions

Place the soy yogurt and banana in your blender and pulse 30 seconds.

Add the cherries, honey, vanilla and the lemon juice and blend until uniform and creamy.

Sprinkle some extra dried berries on top, if desired.

Fruit Coconut Smoothie with Chocolate

(Ready in about 5 minutes | Servings 1)

Ingredients

1 frozen banana

1/2 cup frozen cherries

2 tablespoons shredded coconut

1 tablespoon chocolate syrup

1/3 cup coconut water

Chocolate curls for garnish

Directions

Mix first five ingredients until creamy.

Pour into a tall glass, and top with some extra chocolate curls! Drink with a bendy straw and enjoy!

Green Tea Coconut Smoothie

(Ready in about 5 minutes | Servings 2)

Ingredients

1/2 cup strong green tea

1/4 cup coconut milk

1 cup frozen pineapple

1 frozen banana

1 large frozen grapefruit peeled

1/4 cup frozen baby spinach, frozen

4-5 large ice cubes

1 teaspoon protein powder

Directions

Add green tea and coconut milk to your blender. Then add remaining ingredients.

Mix well, until all ingredients are well blended.

Divide among two glasses. Enjoy!

Flavored Green Tea with Fruits

(Ready in about 15 minutes | Servings 3)

Ingredients

4 green tea bags

1 ½ cups boiling soy milk

1 tablespoon maple syrup

4 frozen kiwis, cubed peeled

2 frozen bananas, cut into chunks

1 teaspoon vanilla extract

Directions

Place the tea bags in a bowl. Pour the soy milk over tea bags, and allow to stand for 3 minutes.

Discard the tea bags. Add chilled tea to the blender. Stir in maple syrup, kiwis, bananas, and vanilla extract. Blend until smooth and uniform. Pour into the glasses and serve.

Light Refreshing Cocktail Smoothie

(Ready in about 5 minutes | Servings 1)

Ingredients

1 lime, peeled

5 mint leaves

1 cucumber, quartered

Directions

Mix all ingredients until smooth, or 1 to 2 minutes.

Pour into a glass and enjoy!

Summer Veggie Smoothie

(Ready in about 5 minutes | Servings 3)

Ingredients

1 tomato

2 radishes with greens

1 yellow bell pepper, de-stemmed

2 stalks celery

1 cucumber

1/2 cup water

Sea salt (optional)

Directions

Combine all of the ingredients in your blender.

Blend well until the vegetables are puréed.

Pour into chilled glasses and enjoy!

Delicious Recovery Smoothie

(Ready in about 5 minutes | Servings 3)

Ingredients

1 grapefruit, peeled and seeded

1 plum, pitted

1 banana, peeled

2 cups spinach

1/4 cup water

Directions

Blend until the smoothie reaches your desired consistency.

Pour into a glass and drink immediately.

This smoothie is an excellent source of vitamin C, fibers, minerals, etc.

Spiced Potato with Tomatoes

(Ready in about 5 minutes | Servings 3)

Ingredients

1 boiled potato

1 scallion

1 red bell pepper, de-stemmed

1/4 teaspoon black pepper

2 tomatoes

1 pinch paprika

Directions

In a blender container, combine all of the ingredients.

Process the ingredients until a smooth consistency develops.

Pour into three glasses and garnish with chives or parsley sprigs, if desired.

Skinny Veggie Smoothie

(Ready in about 5 minutes | Servings 2)

Ingredients

2 scallions

1/4 pound wheatgrass

2 sprigs cilantro

2 tomatoes

1 lime, peeled

1/2 cup water

Directions

Put all of the ingredients into a blender. Blend until the smoothie reaches a desired consistency.

Pour into glasses and drink immediately.

This smoothie is low in calories and good for body cleansing.

Cabbage and Carrot with Tomatoes

(Ready in about 5 minutes | Servings 2)

Ingredients

1/4 head green cabbage

1 medium carrot, quartered

1 clove garlic, peeled

6–8 basil leaves

1 tomato

1 green bell pepper, de-stemmed

2 tablespoons fresh parsley

Directions

Place all of the ingredients in a blender.

Blend ingredients well.

Pour into two glasses and serve.

Simply Exotic Smoothie

(Ready in about 5 minutes | Servings 3)

Ingredients

1 orange, peeled

1 banana, peeled

1/2 cup almond milk

Directions

Add all ingredients to a smoothie maker (blender) and mix until uniform and smooth.

Pour into chilled glasses. Top with whipped cream and drizzle the chocolate syrup if desired. Drink with a bendy straw and enjoy!

Orange Veggies with Greek Yogurt

(Ready in about 10 minutes | Servings 3)

Ingredients

2 sweet potatoes, cut into 1-inch pieces

2 carrots, quartered

1 cup cantaloupe, peeled and seeded

1 cup Greek yogurt

1/2 teaspoon vanilla extract

1/4 teaspoon cinnamon

1 teaspoon raw honey

1/2 cup crushed ice

Directions

Toss all of the ingredients into your blender.

Cover with the lid and blend until smooth.

Pour into the glasses and sprinkle some extra cinnamon on top, if desired.

Green Energy Smoothie

(Ready in about 5 minutes | Servings 3)

Ingredients

1 cup spinach

2 apples, cored and quartered

1 cucumber, quartered

1 banana, peeled

1 scoop vanilla Greek yogurt

1 tablespoon flax seeds

Directions

Put all of the ingredients into a blender container.

Blend until all ingredients are well combined.

Pour into three glasses and garnish with slices of banana or apple (optional).

Tropical Smoothie with Almonds

(Ready in about 5 minutes | Servings 3)

Ingredients

1/4 pineapple, peeled

1/2 cup orange juice

4 medium strawberries, capped

1/2 cup almond milk

Toasted chopped almonds for garnish

Directions

Put all of the ingredients into a blender. Blend until the smoothie reaches a desired consistency.

Pour into three glasses and drink immediately.

This delicious smoothie is a great source of Vitamin C.

Apple Pear Fizz

(Ready in about 5 minutes | Servings 2)

Ingredients

2 apples, cored and quartered

1 pear, cored and quartered

1/2 inch slice ginger

1 cup sparkling water

Directions

Put all of the ingredients into your blender. Blend until the smoothie reaches your desired consistency.

Pour into the glasses. Drink with a bendy straw and enjoy!

Vitamin Boosting Smoothie

(Ready in about 5 minutes | Servings 3)

Ingredients

1 cup broccoli florets

1 cup spinach

1 pear, cored and quartered

6 kale leaves

1 banana, peeled

Directions

Place all of the ingredients in a blender container.

Blend until all ingredients are well combined.

Pour into the glasses and serve.

Pomegranate and Berries with Kiwi

(Ready in about 5 minutes | Servings 3)

Ingredients

1 cup pomegranate seeds

1/2 cup cherries, pitted

2 kiwis, peeled

1/2 cup blackberries

2 beets

1/2 cup water

Directions

Put all of the ingredients into a blender. Blend until the smoothie reaches a desired consistency.

Pour into three glasses and drink immediately.

Plum Banana Protein Smoothie

(Ready in about 5 minutes | Servings 3)

Ingredients

1 plum, pitted

1 banana, peeled

1 scoop whey protein

1 tablespoon flax seeds

1 cup water

1/2 cup ice cubes

Directions

Put all ingredients into a smoothie maker (blender).

Blend until smoothie consistency is reached.

Divide among three glasses. Drink with a bendy straw and enjoy!

Chocolate, Banana and Oats

(Ready in about 5 minutes | Servings 2)

Ingredients

1 scoop whey protein

1 banana, peeled

1/2 cup rolled oats

2 tablespoons almond butter

1 tablespoon cocoa powder

1 cup water

Directions

Blend all ingredients together.

Pour into the chilled glasses. Drizzle the chocolate syrup on top (optional) and drink immediately.

Cabbage Stew Smoothie

(Ready in about 5 minutes | Servings 3)

Ingredients

2 green bell peppers, de-stemmed

3 spring onions

1/4 head cabbage

1/2 jalapeño pepper, de-stemmed

2 stalks celery

2 carrots

1/2 cup tomato juice

1/2 teaspoon cayenne pepper

Salt to taste

Water, if desired

Directions

Place all ingredients in your blender.

Blend until smoothie consistency is reached.

Pour into three glasses and enjoy.

Veggie Afternoon Refresher

(Ready in about 5 minutes | Servings 3)

Ingredients

1 carrot with greens

1 yellow beet

2 celery stalks

1 cucumber, quartered

1 yellow bell pepper, de-stemmed

2 tablespoons basil leaves

1 tablespoon sprouts

Directions

Put all of the ingredients into a blender container. Put lid on tightly.

Pulse until smoothie consistency is reached.

Serve in the glasses and sprinkle some extra sprouts on top.

Veggie Recovery Smoothie

(Ready in about 5 minutes | Servings 3)

Ingredients

1 red potato, cooked

1 cucumber, quartered

1 carrot

1 cup kale

1 yellow squash

1 cup broccoli florets

2 tablespoons fresh parsley

Directions

In your blender, combine the ingredients and purée until the smoothie develops the desired consistency.

Divide among three glasses and serve.

Delicious Kid-Friendly Smoothie

(Ready in about 5 minutes | Servings 2)

Ingredients

1 cup cantaloupe, peeled and seeded

1 carrot with greens

2 apricots, pitted

1/2 cup broccoli florets

4-6 leaves fresh basil

Directions

In a blender, combine ingredients and purée until the smoothie develops your desired consistency.

Divide among three glasses and serve. Drink with a bendy straw and enjoy!

Pineapple Plum Smoothie

(Ready in about 5 minutes | Servings 3)

Ingredients

1/4 pineapple, cut into 1-inch pieces

2 plums, seeded

1 cup sour cherries, pitted

1/2 beet

1/2 cup milk

Directions

Place all ingredients in a smoothie maker (blender).

Blend until smoothie consistency is reached.

Divide among three glasses.

Cantaloupe Apricot Smoothie

(Ready in about 5 minutes | Servings 2)

Ingredients

1 cup cantaloupe, peeled and seeded

1 carrot, with or without the greens

2 apricots, pitted

1/2 cup broccoli florets

1 tablespoon chia seeds

Directions

Place all of the ingredients in a blender.

Blend until smooth and uniform.

Pour into glasses and sprinkle with fresh mint, if desired.

Spring Garden Smoothie

(Ready in about 5 minutes | Servings 3)

Ingredients

1 zucchini

1 cucumber, quartered

1 yellow or red bell pepper, de-stemmed

2 sprigs dill

1/2 cup water

2 tablespoons fresh parsley

1 tablespoon cilantro

Directions

In a smoothie maker (blender), mix all ingredients until smooth.

Divide among glasses. Drink with a bendy straw and enjoy!

Potato Soup Smoothie

(Ready in about 10 minutes | Servings 4)

Ingredients

2 potatoes, peeled and cooked

2-3 spring onions

3 sprigs parsley

2 cups baby spinach

1 teaspoon rosemary

1 cup water

Directions

Place all ingredients in a blender.

Blend until smoothie consistency is reached.

Divide among chilled glasses.

Skin Rejuvenating Smoothie

(Ready in about 5 minutes | Servings 3)

Ingredients

1 orange, peeled

1 cup passion fruit

1 cup blackberries

1 carrot with greens

Directions

In a blender container, combine ingredients and purée until smooth and thick.

Pour into glasses and drink immediately.

Veggie and Lemongrass with Spices

(Ready in about 5 minutes | Servings 3)

Ingredients

1 cucumber, quartered

1 cup arugula

1 carrot with greens

1/2 sweet potato

1/4 pound lemongrass

1/4 teaspoon ground cinnamon

1/4 teaspoon grated nutmeg

Directions

Put all of the ingredients into your blender.

Mix until smooth and creamy.

Pour into glasses and sprinkle some extra cinnamon over the top. Enjoy!

Breakfast-to-Go Smoothie

(Ready in about 5 minutes | Servings 2)

Ingredients

2 cups mixed berries

2 carrots

1 cup wheatgrass

1 teaspoon cinnamon

1/2 cup water

Directions

Place all ingredients in a blender.

Cover and blend until smooth, creamy and uniform.

Divide your smoothie among two chilled glasses.

Banana Ice Cream Smoothie

(Ready in about 10 minutes | Servings 4)

Ingredients

1 banana, peeled

2 scoops vanilla ice cream

1 cup milk

2 egg white

Directions

Place all ingredients in your smoothie maker.

Mix well until smoothie consistency is reached.

Pour into glasses, sprinkle with coconut flakes or chocolate curls and serve.

Berry and Banana with Cottage Cheese

(Ready in about 10 minutes | Servings 2)

Ingredients

1/2 cup mixed frozen berries

1/2 frozen banana

1/2 cup low-fat cottage cheese

1 cup almond milk

Chopped toasted almonds for garnish

Directions

Place first four ingredients in your blender.

Mix until everything is blended.

Pour into chilled glasses, garnish with chopped almonds and enjoy!

Delicious Low Carb Smoothie

(Ready in about 10 minutes | Servings 2)

Ingredients

1 cup whole milk

1/2 cup fat-free cottage cheese

1 scoop whey protein

1 teaspoon raw honey

1/4 teaspoon vanilla extract

1/8 teaspoon ground cinnamon

1/8 teaspoon ground nutmeg

1/2 cup crushed ice

Directions

Pulse the milk and cottage cheese first until the cottage is creamy.

Add the rest of ingredients and blend until smooth and uniform.

Pour into a chilled glass! Add your favorite sprinkles on top and enjoy!

Banana and Peach with Cottage Cheese

(Ready in about 10 minutes | Servings 2)

Ingredients

1 banana

1/2 cup peach

1 cup skim milk

1/3 cup cottage cheese

1 teaspoon almond extract

Directions

Add all ingredients to a smoothie maker (blender) and mix until everything is well blended.

Pour into chilled glasses and serve.

Fruit with Cottage Cheese and Greek Yogurt

(Ready in about 5 minutes | Servings 1)

Ingredients

2 carrots, quartered

1/2 cup fresh pineapple, peeled and chopped

6 ounces Greek yogurt

1/4 cup cottage cheese

1 teaspoon honey

Directions

In a blender, combine all of the ingredients.

Cover with the lid and blend until smooth and creamy.

Pour into two glass, garnish with some extra chopped walnuts (optional) and serve.

Drink with a bendy straw and enjoy!

Best Protein Breakfast Smoothie

(Ready in about 5 minutes | Servings 1)

Ingredients

1/2 cup milk

1/2 cup fat-free plain yogurt

1/2 frozen banana

1/2 cup frozen strawberries

2 tablespoons protein supplement powder

1 teaspoon agave syrup or maple syrup

Directions

Combine all ingredients in a blender. Pulse until the mixture becomes smooth and creamy.

Pour into a chilled glass and serve immediately.

Iced Mocha Smoothie

(Ready in about 5 minutes | Servings 1)

Ingredients

3/4 cup milk

3 tablespoons granulated sugar

3 tablespoons mocha flavored instant coffee mix

1 cup crushed ice

Directions

In a blender or a food processor, combine all of the ingredients.

Mix until smooth. Pour into a chilled glass.

Drizzle the chocolate syrup on top or serve alongside the dark chocolate (optional).

Drink with a bendy straw! Enjoy!

Mango, Banana and Orange

(Ready in about 10 minutes | Servings 4)

Ingredients

1 mango - peeled, seeded, and cut into chunks

1 banana, peeled and chopped

1 cup orange juice

1 cup vanilla nonfat yogurt

Directions

Combine all ingredients in a blender.

Pulse until the mixture becomes smooth and creamy.

Pour into chilled glasses and serve immediately. Drink with a bendy straw and enjoy!

Strawberries with Lemon Yogurt and Orange

(Ready in about 10 minutes | Servings 1)

Ingredients

8-10 strawberries

1 cup lemon yogurt

1/3 cup orange juice

Directions

In a blender container, combine ingredients and purée until your smoothie develops the desired consistency.

Pour into a glass and serve immediately.

Almond and Chocolate Banana Smoothie

(Ready in about 10 minutes | Servings 1)

Ingredients

1 banana, sliced

1/2 cup skim milk

1 tablespoon almond butter

2 tablespoons chocolate syrup

Directions

In a blender container, combine ingredients and purée until your smoothie develops the desired consistency.

Pour into a tall glass and drizzle some extra chocolate syrup.

Vodka Orange Smoothie

(Alcoholic | Ready in about 10 minutes | Servings 4)

Ingredients

6 fluid ounces vodka

18 fluid ounces orange juice

1 cup frozen strawberries

4 scoops orange sherbet

1 cup crushed ice

Directions

Put all of the ingredients into a blender container.

Mix well, until all ingredients are well blended.

Divide among four glasses and serve!

Amaretto Vanilla Smoothie

(Alcoholic | Ready in about 10 minutes | Servings 4)

Ingredients

4 (1.5 fluid ounce) jiggers amaretto liqueur

4 (1.5 fluid ounce) jiggers milk

1 cup vanilla ice cream

Crushed ice for garnish

Directions

Add all of the ingredients to your blender. Blend until smooth and frothy.

Pour over crushed ice and serve.

Summer Pina Colada

(Alcoholic | Ready in about 10 minutes | Servings 1)

Ingredients

3/4 cup fresh pineapple

1/2 banana

1/4 cup coconut milk

1 ½ ounces rum

1/4 cup crushed ice

Directions

Put all ingredients into your blender.

Blend well until smoothie consistency is reached.

Pour into two chilled glasses. Enjoy!

Banana Baileys Smoothie

(Alcoholic | Ready in about 10 minutes | Servings 2)

Ingredients

4 ripe bananas, cut into chunks

1 cup plain yogurt

2-3 tablespoons Baileys Irish Cream

2 tablespoons sugar

½ cup peanut butter

20 ice cubes

Directions

Add all ingredients (except the ice cubes) to the blender.

Continue to blend and gradually add the ice cubes.

Pour into glasses and serve.

Festive Eggnog Smoothie

(Alcoholic | Ready in about 2 hours 10 minutes | Servings 8)

Ingredients

4 cups eggnog

1 (5.1 ounce) package instant vanilla pudding
mix

1 ½ cups frozen whipped topping

1/2 cup rum

Directions

Combine all ingredients in a blender. Pulse until the mixture becomes smooth and creamy.

Refrigerate at least 2 hours.

Pour into glasses and serve chilled.

Banana and Chocolate Milk Smoothie

(Ready in about 10 minutes | Servings 2)

Ingredients

1 frozen banana

1 tablespoon cocoa powder

¾ cup chocolate milk

Whipped cream for garnish

Directions

In a blender, combine banana, cocoa powder and chocolate milk. Blend until creamy and smooth.

Pour into two chilled glasses and top with whipped cream.

Sprinkle some extra cocoa powder and serve. Drink with a bendy straw and enjoy!

Fruit with Chocolate Hazelnut Milk

(Ready in about 10 minutes | Servings 2)

Ingredients

2 ripe frozen bananas, cut into chunks

1 ripe pear, cored and quartered

1 cup chocolate hazelnut milk

Whipped cream for garnish (optional)

Sprinkles of choice (optional)

Directions

Combine all of the ingredients in a blender container.

Cover and blend until creamy and smooth.

Divide among two chilled glasses. Top with whipped cream and add your favorite sprinkles.

Avocado Strawberry Cocoa Smoothie

(Ready in about 5 minutes | Servings 2)

Ingredients

1 ripe avocado

1 cup frozen strawberries

1 ½ cups milk

1/2 teaspoon vanilla

1 tablespoon cocoa powder

1 teaspoon maple syrup

Directions

Place all ingredients in your blender.

Blend until smoothie consistency is reached.

Pour into two glasses and enjoy. Garnish with chocolate shavings if desired.

Mint Avocado Spinach Smoothie

(Ready in about 5 minutes | Servings 1)

Ingredients

1/2 avocado

1/2 cup spinach

3/4 cup Greek yogurt

1 cup milk

5 ice cubes

1 teaspoon raw honey

1/4 teaspoon mint extract

Directions

In a blender container, combine ingredients and purée until smooth and uniform.

Pour into a tall glass. Sprinkle with chocolate curls and drink with a bendy straw.

Morning Coffee Smoothie

(Ready in about 10 minutes | Servings 4)

Ingredients

2 tablespoons instant coffee

2 tablespoons hot water

2 cups vanilla ice cream

1/4 cup powdered chocolate milk mix

1 ½ cups milk

Directions

In a blender container, combine ingredients and purée until smooth.

Divide among four glasses. Add your favorite sprinkles and enjoy!

Download a FREE PDF file with photos of all the recipes by following the link:

Made in the USA
Middletown, DE
09 March 2017